THE MIGHTY PAUL
*Robeson*

# THE SONG OF FREEDOM

The World's Greatest
Singer in the Finest
Film Production of his
Career

*Directed by*
J. ELDER WILLS

A British Lion–Hammer Production

BRITISH LION FILM CORP. LTD., 76-78, WARDOUR STREET, W.I

# GRANDPA
## STOPS A WAR

# GRANDPA STOPS A WAR

## A PAUL ROBESON STORY

### SUSAN ROBESON
### ROD BROWN

ILLUSTRATED BY

7 SEVEN STORIES

TRIANGLE SQUARE
books for young readers

NEW YORK • OAKLAND

ROD BROWN'S ACKNOWLEDGMENTS

*I would like to dedicate this book to my wife, Cathy Elaine Brown,*
*the daughter of Edith Nancy Bray-Barton, the daughter of Aretta Mickens-Thompson.*

SUSAN ROBESON'S ACKNOWLEDGMENTS

*Dedicated to Paul Robeson Jr. and Marilyn Robeson, David Paul Robeson, and Emanuel Quintero Robeson.*
*Special thanks to my literary agent, Marie Dutton Brown, for her wisdom and guidance—couldn't have done it without you.*
*Heartfelt appreciation to Dan Simon and the Seven Stories team for their spirit of collaboration and belief in this story.*

Text copyright © 2019 Susan Robeson / Illustrations © 2019 Rod Brown

A TRIANGLE SQUARE BOOKS FOR YOUNG READERS FIRST EDITION

SEVEN STORIES PRESS
140 Watt Street, New York, NY 10013
www.sevenstories.com

LIBRARY OF CONGRESS CATALOGING-IN-PUBLICATION DATA

Names: Robeson, Susan, 1953- author.   Brown, Rod, 1961- illustrator.
Title: Grandpa stops a war : a Paul Robeson story / Susan Robeson ; illustrated by Rod Brown.
Other titles: Paul Robeson story
Description: First edition.   New York : Seven Stories Press, [2018]
Audience: Grades K-3.   Audience: Ages 5-9.
Identifiers: LCCN 2018045391  ISBN 9781609808822 (hardcover)  ISBN 9781609808839 (ebook)
Subjects: LCSH: Robeson, Paul, 1898-1976--Juvenile literature.   African
Americans--Biography--Juvenile literature.   Singers--United States--Biography--Juvenile literature.
Peace--Juvenile literature.   Spain--History--Civil War, 1936-1939--African Americans--Juvenile
literature.   Spain--History--Civil War, 1936-1939--Participation, African Americans--Juvenile literature.
Actors--United States--Biography--Juvenile literature.   Political activists--United States--Biography--Juvenile literature.
Classification: LCC E185.97.R63 R59 2018   DDC 782.0092 [B] --dc23
LC record available at https://lccn.loc.gov/2018045391

Printed in Canada

1 3 5 7 9 8 6 4 2

Daddy always said it takes a man of peace to stop a war. And that's just what my Grandpa Paul did. He stopped a war.

When I was a little girl, I always asked my father to tell me this story.

"Grandpa Paul stopped a war," Daddy would say.

"But, Daddy, how could he do that? He's not a general or a president. He's a singer."

6

Daddy would tell me the story while our family was taking a car trip to our favorite lake.

First he would tell me how special Grandpa Paul was, and
each time he added something new.

Grandpa Paul was very tall and very handsome. His deep voice rumbled like thunder, but he never frightened people because he was so kind. Grandpa was a gentle giant. And children loved him because he always had time to play.

Grandpa Paul was one of the greatest singers in the world. His favorite songs were African American spirituals.

Africans sang the spirituals after they were kidnapped and brought to America as slaves. They used secret codes in the songs to help people know when to escape.

Grandpa Paul's father was a slave in North Carolina. When he was only fifteen years old, he escaped to freedom because he knew the secret codes.

Many years later, he taught the songs to Grandpa Paul. When Grandpa Paul sang these songs to people all over the world they understood what Grandpa felt in his heart even though they didn't speak the same language.

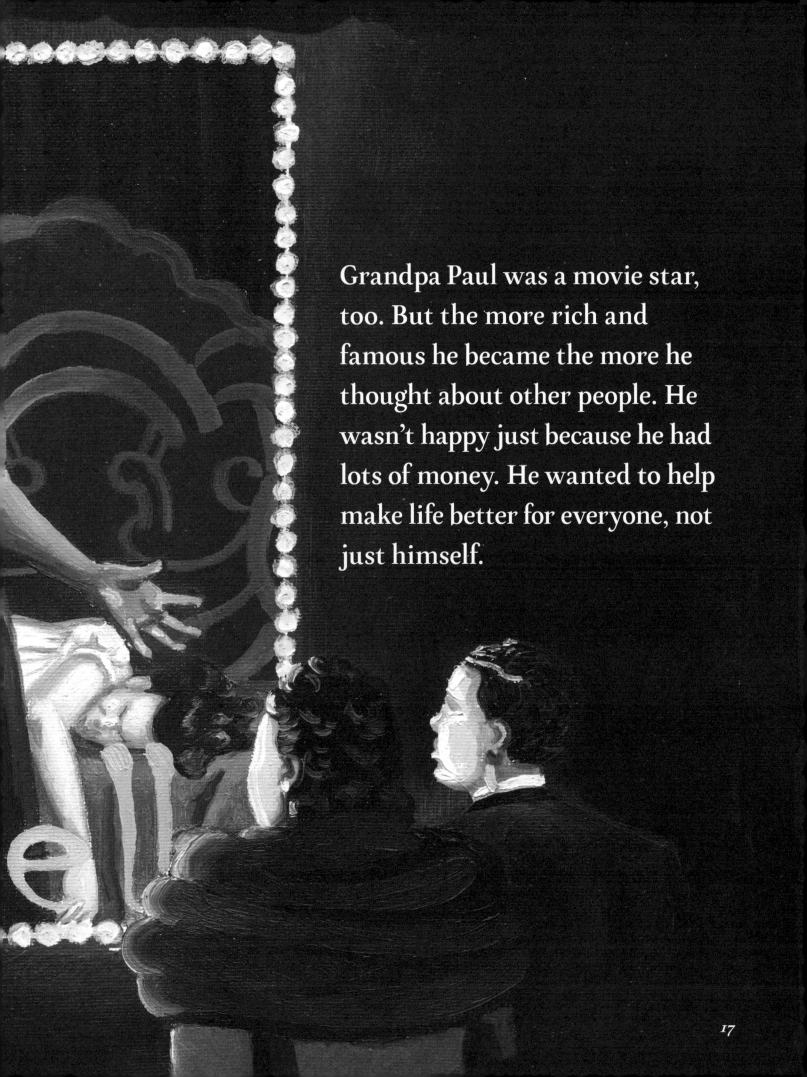

Grandpa Paul was a movie star, too. But the more rich and famous he became the more he thought about other people. He wasn't happy just because he had lots of money. He wanted to help make life better for everyone, not just himself.

While Grandpa Paul was living in London, war broke out in a nearby country called Spain. Generals in the Spanish Army had taken over the government and started a war.

Many children in Spain didn't have enough food to eat or clothes to keep them warm. Many families were homeless because bombs were destroying their villages and cities.

Grandpa Paul decided to help. So he sang.

Thousands of people came to his concerts in London. They brought money and food and clothes to send to children in Spain. Grandpa felt good when he sent everything to them.

But the war
in Spain continued
and got worse. More and more
children and their families were suffering.

Grandpa Paul decided to go to Spain. He didn't know what he would do or how he would help, he just knew he had to do more.

Grandpa Paul's friends and family got very upset.

"It's too dangerous," Nana told him. "Stay in London where it's safe. You can do plenty from here."

"But I need to do more," Grandpa Paul said.

"Why risk your life?" his friends asked. "You're not Spanish."

"Because wherever there is war people suffer," Paul said. "And each of us must do our part to bring peace into the world."

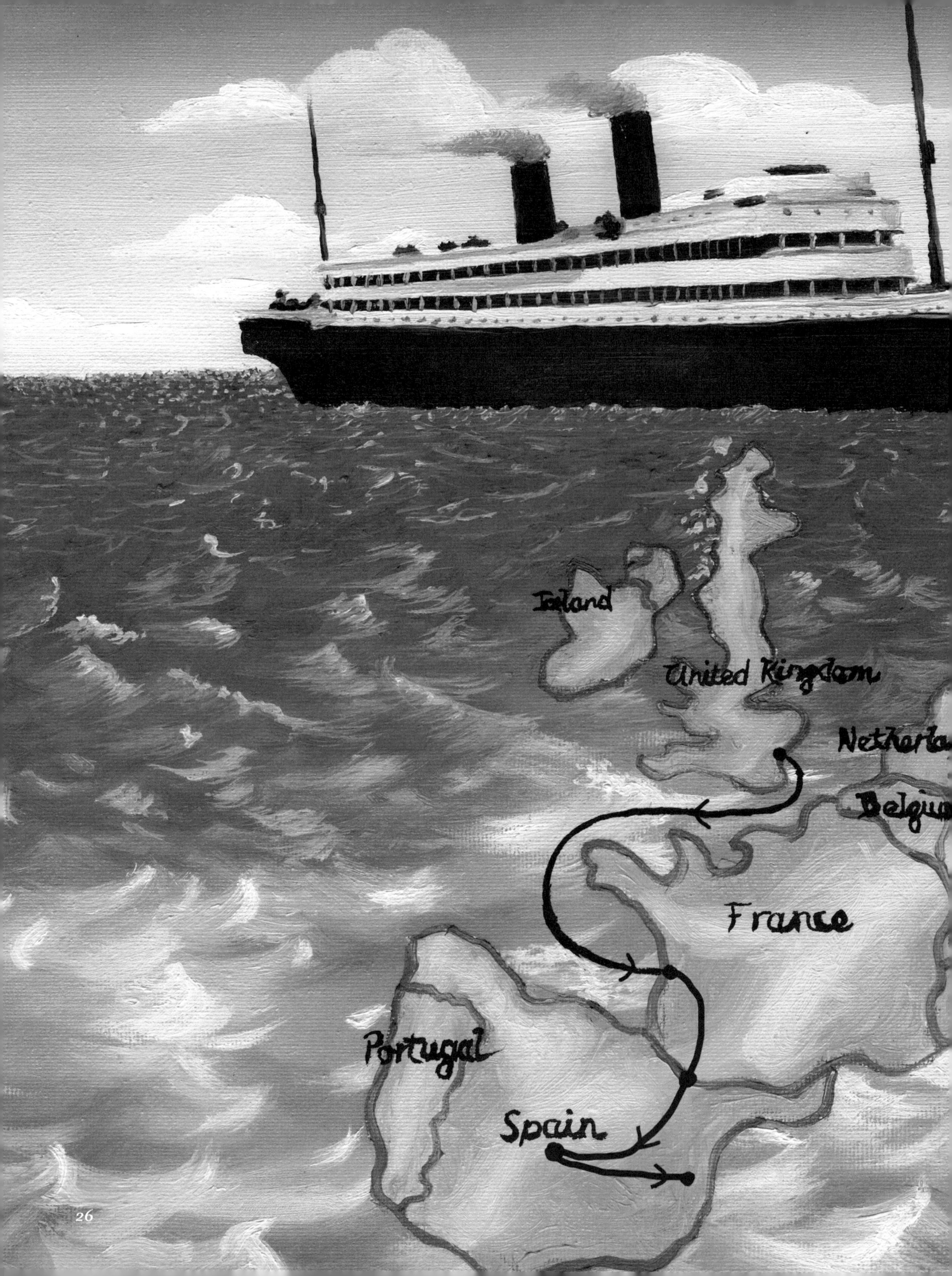

Iceland

United Kingdom

Netherla

Belgiu

France

Portugal

Spain

"You're only a singer. What can you do?" they replied.

"I don't know," Grandpa Paul said, "but I know I must go."

"If you're going," Nana said, "I'm going too."

So Grandpa and Nana went to Spain.

Switzerland

The first night they were in Madrid, the city was bombed. The windows in their hotel shattered and the whole building shook. There were no lights and everyone huddled together while planes flew overhead dropping bombs. Then someone said, "Let's sing!"

As everyone sang, their fear melted away.

That gave Grandpa Paul an idea. He asked his Spanish
friends to take him to the front lines of the war, where a
big battle was taking place.

"It's too dangerous!" they all said at once.

Grandpa Paul insisted.

Grandpa Paul's Spanish friend, Captain Fernando, drove him to Teruel, where the fighting was fierce. They drove through the hills and valleys of the countryside, past miles of olive trees and through groves of Valencia oranges that looked like little suns against the sad landscape.

As Captain Fernando and Grandpa neared the front lines of
Teruel, the gunfire was so loud they couldn't hear each other talk.

They passed a big crater in the road where a bomb had just
fallen. Captain Fernando looked over to see if Grandpa Paul
was afraid to go on.

"Keep driving," Grandpa Paul said. "I want to sing my songs."

Captain Fernando was surprised. "In the middle of a war?"

"Yes," Grandpa Paul said. "I especially want to sing where men are fighting. Maybe my songs will give them hope for a peaceful world."

It was a cold afternoon in 1938 when Grandpa Paul arrived in Teruel.

The men fighting to save the Spanish republic were discouraged. They were hungry. They were cold and many were injured.

When the men saw Grandpa Paul their spirits lifted. They couldn't believe he had traveled so far and through so much danger to be with them.

"Please sing for us," they shouted with joy. They didn't care that war was all around them. They just wanted to hear Grandpa Paul sing.

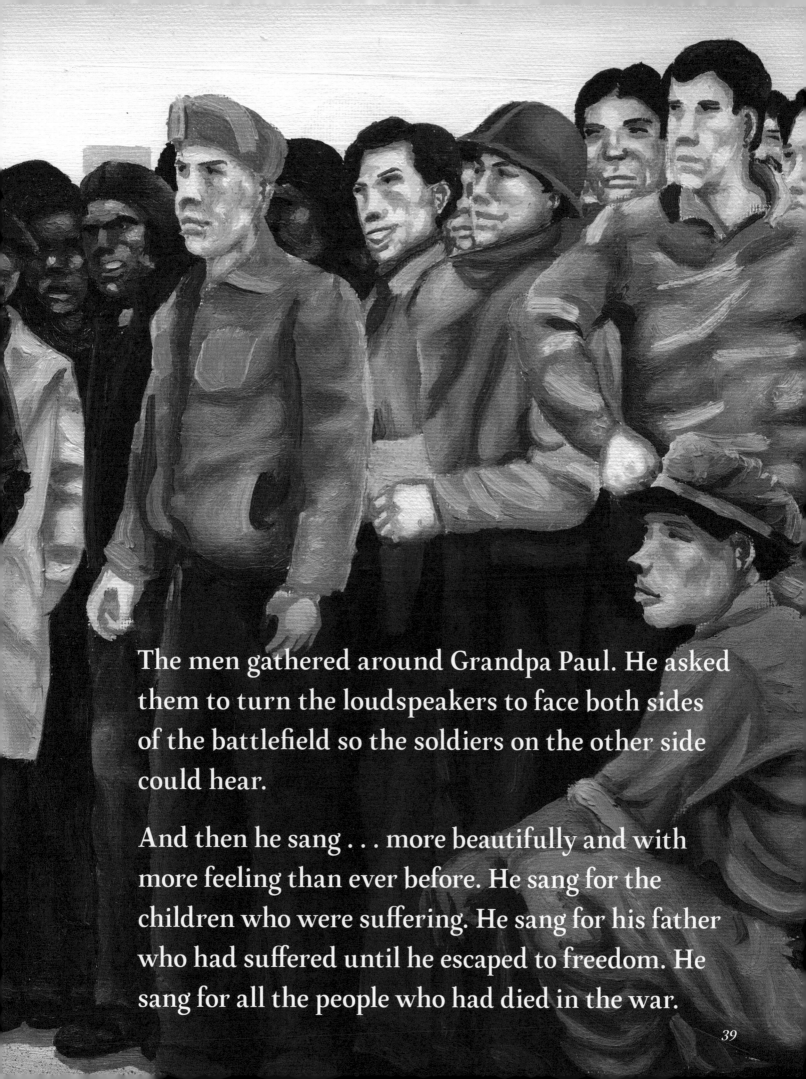

The men gathered around Grandpa Paul. He asked them to turn the loudspeakers to face both sides of the battlefield so the soldiers on the other side could hear.

And then he sang . . . more beautifully and with more feeling than ever before. He sang for the children who were suffering. He sang for his father who had suffered until he escaped to freedom. He sang for all the people who had died in the war.

The battlefield grew silent.

No shots were fired.

No bombs fell.

There was just Grandpa Paul's rumbling voice singing African American spirituals and songs of peace and love and freedom.

While Grandpa Paul sang
there was peace.

# Author's Note

**GRANDPA STOPS A WAR** tells the story of four powers that shaped my childhood as a Robeson: the power of music to move hearts and minds, the courage to act according to your beliefs, the artist as a citizen of the world, and the power of compassion. I learned what it means to be free and stand up for what you believe in. Eventually, I developed a personal code, a set of values to guide my life. Today, popular culture equates money, celebrity, and professional standing with power. Real power resides in our personal values, and we learn these from our families.

**GRANDPA STOPS A WAR** shows and tells how families pass down stories, making past experiences come alive and become a part of the present. When my father told our family stories to my brother and me, my grandfather became my guide into history, of the past and the present, and I became part of it.

*Everyone's family stories have power—if you share them.*

## THE SPANISH CIVIL WAR (1936–1939)

After Paul Robeson sang on the front lines, the Republicans in Spain (the Loyalists) fighting to save their country's democracy won the battle at Teruel, but a year later they lost the war. With military support from Italy and Nazi Germany, General Franco proved too powerful. His military government ruled Spain for the next thirty-six years, until his death in 1975.

Over 35,000 volunteers from fifty-two nations defied travel bans and traveled to Spain to help save the democratically elected Spanish republic from fascism, including more than 2,500 Americans who formed the Abraham Lincoln Battalion. Doctors and nurses drove ambulances and performed surgery in makeshift hospitals. Writers Ernest Hemingway, Martha Gellhorn, Langston Hughes and

Robeson family portrait, New York, 1957. Bottom row, left to right: author, Paul Robeson (Grandpa Paul), author's brother David Robeson. Top row left to right: author's mother Marilyn Robeson, author's grandmother Eslanda Robeson (Nana), author's father Paul Robeson Jr. (Daddy).

photographer Robert Capa were among those who went to Spain to report the story. The artist Pablo Picasso painted *Guernica*, one of his most famous works, decrying the Nazi bombing of that Spanish village. Ordinary people from England and France delivered relief aid to families in Spain who had become refugees in their own country. Paul went even though he didn't believe in solving world problems by war—the Spanish people had no other choice to defend their democracy. And he had come to believe that artists have a responsibility to speak out about injustice in the world—and do something.

### ESLANDA ROBESON (NANA)

My grandmother, Eslanda, finally did go to Spain with Paul despite her initial opposition to the trip. She feared Paul would ruin his career or be killed, and his safety was first and foremost. The trip to Spain with Paul transformed Eslanda as she experienced the terrors of war and witnessed the bravery of men, women, and children from all walks of life. She returned to London more politically engaged and supportive of Paul's tireless activism.

## CAPTAIN FERNANDO CASTILLO (CAPTAIN FERNANDO)

When the Republicans lost the war, Paul's military escort, Fernando, made a daring escape on foot through the Pyrenees into France. Months later, the doorbell of my grandparents' London apartment rang. My father, then ten years old, opened the door; there stood Fernando, exhausted and starving. My grandparents gave him refuge and helped him regain his health. Over the next few months, Paul and Eslanda helped Fernando locate his two older brothers and father-in-law and bring them to London, then resettled them in Mexico. However, Fernando's sisters and mother suffered many years in Franco's prisons. Fernando and my grandparents remained lifelong friends.

Paul Robeson, center, with men of the International Brigade and the Abraham Lincoln Battalion. Photo by Eslanda G. Robeson, 1938.

PAUL ROBESON (1898–1976), the son of a fugitive slave and free Black woman of Quaker and Lenni Lenape descent, was one of the most acclaimed men of the twentieth century. He broke barriers and set records as an athlete, scholar, singer and actor when segregation was still the law.

Considered one of the twentieth century's greatest voices, Robeson spoke and sang in over fifteen languages. Most famously known for his rendition of "Ol' Man River," by the early 1940s Robeson was a household name. Notably, he refused to let his fame and wealth as a singer and actor blind him to the suffering of others. An early forerunner of the civil rights movement, Robeson also championed economic justice, global freedom movements, and world peace. Among Robeson's friends and admirers were President Franklin Roosevelt, Pablo Picasso, Jawaharlal Nehru, Oscar Hammerstein, James Baldwin, and Nelson Mandela.

In the late 1940s and '50s, when the Cold War and witch hunts of McCarthyism gripped the nation, Robeson's ideals became "un-American." Most were intimidated into silence, but Robeson continued to speak out. In retaliation, the State Department revoked his passport while the FBI orchestrated a virtual ban. Venues refused to let Robeson perform or record; record stores removed his albums; radio DJs were fired for playing his music; his name was even struck from record books. In 1958, after eight long years, the US Supreme Court declared it unconstitutional to deny citizens the right to travel based on political beliefs. At the age of sixty, Robeson regained his passport, reestablished his career and continued to speak out for freedom and world peace. Paul Robeson remained the quintessential citizen of the world—a man of principle and an inspiration to millions.